That's Wild!

SPIDERS Are ACROBATS!

And other Strange Facts

GARY SPROTT

Rourke
Educational Media
rourkeeducationalmedia.com

A Division of
Carson Dellosa Education

BEFORE AND DURING READING ACTIVITIES

Before Reading: *Building Background Knowledge and Vocabulary*

Building background knowledge can help children process new information and build upon what they already know. Before reading a book, it is important to tap into what children already know about the topic. This will help them develop their vocabulary and increase their reading comprehension.

Questions and Activities to Build Background Knowledge:

1. Look at the front cover of the book and read the title. What do you think this book will be about?
2. What do you already know about this topic?
3. Take a book walk and skim the pages. Look at the table of contents, photographs, captions, and bold words. Did these text features give you any information or predictions about what you will read in this book?

Vocabulary: *Vocabulary Is Key to Reading Comprehension*

Use the following directions to prompt a conversation about each word.

- Read the vocabulary words.
- What comes to mind when you see each word?
- What do you think each word means?

> **Vocabulary Words:**
> - acrobatics
> - ambush
> - arthropods
> - descent
> - protein
> - venom

During Reading: *Reading for Meaning and Understanding*

To achieve deep comprehension of a book, children are encouraged to use close reading strategies. During reading, it is important to have children stop and make connections. These connections result in deeper analysis and understanding of a book.

Close Reading a Text

During reading, have children stop and talk about the following:

- Any confusing parts
- Any unknown words
- Text to text, text to self, text to world connections
- The main idea in each chapter or heading

Encourage children to use context clues to determine the meaning of any unknown words. These strategies will help children learn to analyze the text more thoroughly as they read.

When you are finished reading this book, turn to the next-to-last page for **After Reading Questions** and an **Activity**.

Table of Contents

Wild World of Webs

One spooked Little Miss Muffet while she was snacking. Another bit teenage science geek Peter Parker and turned him into a superhero. Be warned: When it comes to spiders, the facts are just as freaky and fascinating as the nursery rhymes and comic books!

In Every Corner!

There are more than 40,000 species of spiders around the world. These critters can live pretty much anywhere—in deserts, rainforests, underwater, and, of course, in cupboards and closets!

Spiders are arachnids, eight-legged members of the group of animals known as **arthropods**. Do you shriek at the sight of a spider? Perhaps it's a case of arachnophobia—an extremely strong fear of spiders!

arthropods (AHR-thruh-pahds): animals without backbones that have hard outer skeletons and three or more pairs of legs that can bend

Don't worry if you've never spotted a Samoan moss spider. This wee web spinner is the world's smallest spider and almost invisible to the human eye. How tiny is it? About the same size as the period at the end of this sentence.

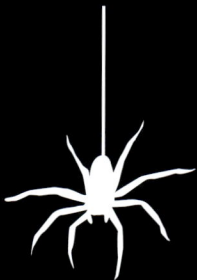

ambush (AM-bush): a trap in which to hide until attack

Not So Itsy-Bitsy!

Guess what the goliath bird-eating spider likes to munch for lunch. Yup, wings—along with the rest of the bird! This humongous hunter is about the size of a dinner plate. It sets an **ambush** for its prey and then bites down with its deadly fangs.

The South American goliath bird-eating spider can weigh as much as a puppy.

Spiders use silk to weave their webs. The silk, a type of **protein**, is created inside the arachnid's body and pushed out through openings known as *spinnerets*. For its size, spider silk is stronger than steel!

protein (PROH-teen): a type of chemical compound found in all living plant and animal cells

Catching a Big Bug!

Orb weaver spiders on the island of Madagascar build webs big enough to cover a Volkswagen Beetle! The spiders can stretch their super-strong silk across rivers. These bridge lines can reach up to 45 feet (14 meters) long!

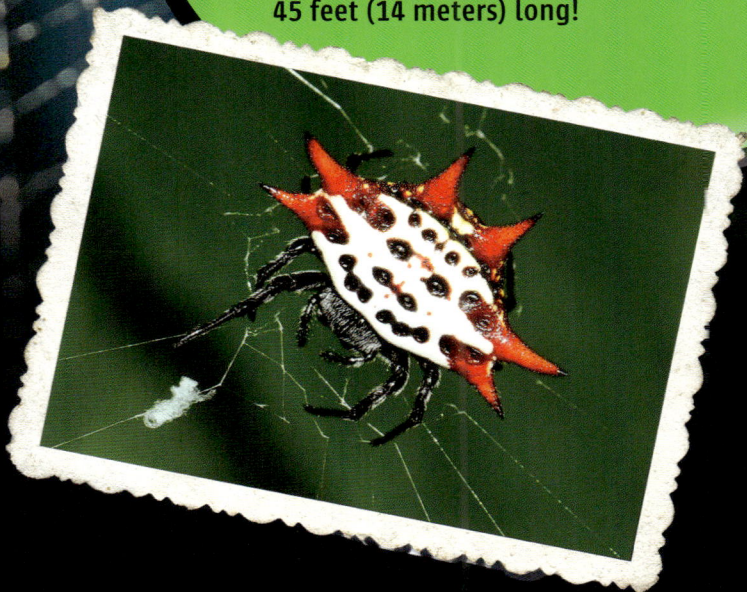

The diving bell spider is the only species of spider that lives almost entirely underwater. This arachnid spins a web between plants below the surface of ponds and streams. The spider then fills its balloon-shaped home with air bubbles trapped by the teensy hairs on its body and legs.

Taking the First Bite

Female spiders can lay up to 2,500 eggs, which they wrap in a silk sac for protection. When it's time for her eggs to hatch, the female wolf spider bites into the sac to release her pack of spiderlings! "Hi, I'm your mom. Hi, I'm your mom. Hi, I'm your mom..."

Spider Superpowers

Eat My Dust, Dude!

In the Sahara Desert in Africa, the spider nicknamed the "flic-flac" escapes predators by flipping through the air! With a running start, this mini-Olympian reaches out with its front legs, spins through midair, and lands on its back legs. This trick allows the flic-flac to double its speed!

Jumping, jigging, flipping, and flying—spiders are masters at **acrobatics**. Arachnids perform these amazing feats to find a mate, snag their food, or avoid becoming another creature's meal!

acrobatics (ak-ruh-BAT-iks): difficult gymnastic acts, often performed in the air or on a high wire

A skydiving spider? Sure, but without a parachute! In tropical rainforests, a type of spider known as a "flattie" glides from treetop to treetop. If it falls or gets blown by wind, this skinny daredevil has a way to control its **descent**. It extends its two front legs in a Superman-like pose and dives to a safe place.

descent (di-SENT): the act of going from a higher to a lower level

Why spin a web when you can pounce like a cat? Some jumping spiders leap up to 40 times their body length—without a running start! With eight eyes, including four on top of their heads, these arachnids have cat-like vision to match their feline leaping ability.

Sparklemuffin Struts Its Stuff!

In Australia, peacock spiders are famous for their colorful markings and leg-shaking, body-rolling mating dances. One species has bright red and blue stripes, and is known as—wait for it—Sparklemuffin!

Hairy, Scary Hunters

They're not much bigger than a paper clip, but black widows are among the scariest of spiders. The female has a red hourglass shape on her belly, and one bite from this deadly arachnid could mean your time is almost up! The black widow's **venom** is thought to be 15 times more powerful than a rattlesnake's.

Shake It Off!

You can see here that the male black widow spider is smaller than the female. What you can't see is that he is scared! Females may eat the males. Yikes! So, the male vibrates its abdomen when it enters the female's web. This booty shake is his way of saying, "I'm your mate, not your meal!"

venom (VEN-uhm): a toxic substance produced by some snakes and spiders; venom is usually passed into a victim's body through a bite or sting

21

Flesh-eating zombies? Ho-hum. How about flesh-killing spider bites? The venom of the brown recluse is wicked! It causes skin and tissue to turn black before falling off. Thank goodness this spider is reclusive, living up to its name. The brown recluse likes to be left alone and out of the way of humans.

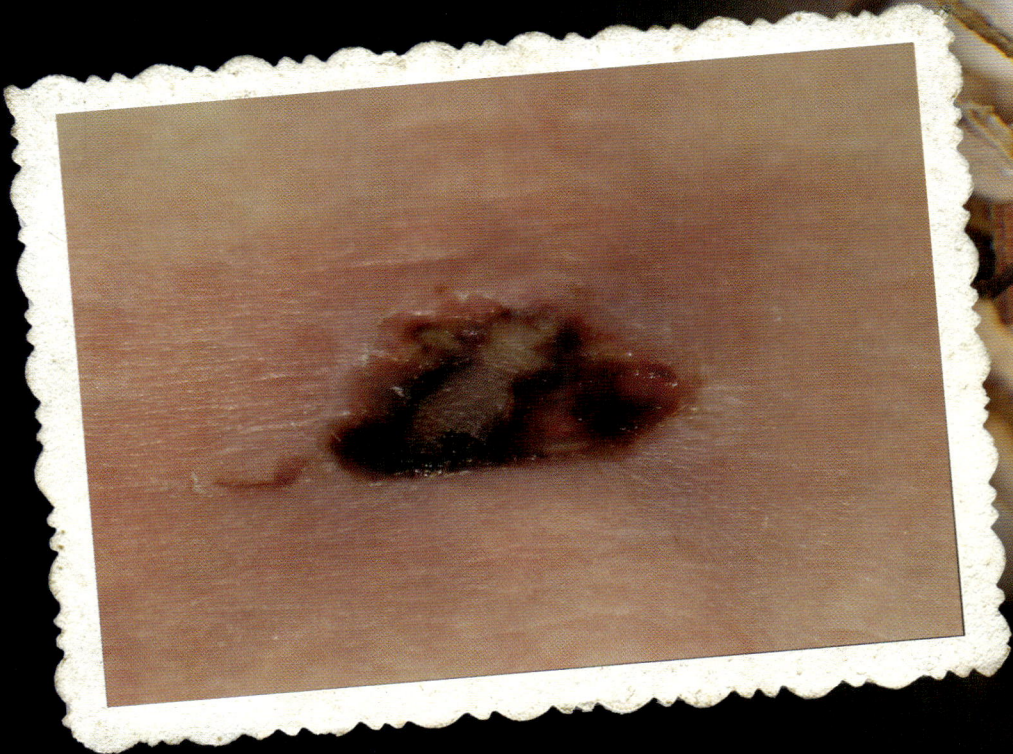

Pain medications and antibiotics are used to treat brown recluse bites. Serious injury and death are rare.

With its big hairy legs and body, the creepy tarantula could make your hair stand on end with fright! This burrowing spider snatches frogs, mice, and insects with its legs and delivers a fatal bite. The tarantula uses digestive juices to turn its prey into liquid that it sucks into its mouth. Hey, don't slurp your mouse-shake!

A tarantula can live for 30 years!

Hair Today, Gone Tomorrow!

A tarantula's hair comes in handy when things get hairy! The spider uses its legs to kick hairs off its belly when threatened. Like miniature darts or arrows, the hairs get stuck in the eyes of the spider's predators.

The ogre-faced spider has a bug-eyed, ugly mug. But it has an elegant way of snaring its prey. It spins a web between its front legs and then hangs upside down from trees or bushes. When an insect passes below, the silk net drops—whoosh!—and dinner is caught!

Something Smells Good!

Bolas spiders prefer line fishing to net fishing. Bolas unspool a long thread of silk with a drop of a sticky substance at the end of the line. The spider also releases an odor that smells like a female moth. If a curious male moth arrives, the bolas swings or throws its line and the winged admirer gets stuck like glue.

Here's a tip: Don't get a spitting spider spitting mad! When hunting, these unique arachnids unleash a squirt of saliva. With its prey now—ew!—stuck in spit, the spider bites down to finish the job.

Memory Game

Look at the pictures. What do you remember reading on the pages where each image appeared?

Index

After Reading Questions

1. How many species of spiders are there around the world?

2. How does a tarantula protect itself from predators?

3. Why does a male black widow shake its abdomen when entering a female's web?

4. How do spiders known as "flatties" move about the rainforest?

5. What is arachnophobia?

Activity

How many books, songs, comics, rhymes, and movies can you think of that are about spiders? Create a list and pick your favorite fictional spiders. Are the spiders good or bad? Do they have special powers?

About the Author

Gary Sprott is a writer in Tampa, Florida. He's pretty good at catching spiders around the house. But he's not sure he has a plastic container big enough if he ever finds a goliath bird-eating spider!

© 2020 Rourke Educational Media

www.rourkeeducationalmedia.com

PHOTO CREDITS: Cover & Title Page ©Pavel Krasensky;Pg 18, 20 ©PK289; Pg 21, 30 ©Cris Ritchie Photo; Pg 25, 30 ©Sebastian Janicki; Pg 27, 30 ©reptiles4all; Pg 4 ©Chuck Wagner; Pg 5 ©Usa-Pyon; Pg 6 ©kali9; Pg 7 ©ChristinaPrinn; Pg 9 ©The Reptilarium; Pg 11 ©Roberto; Pg 11 ©Chuck Wagner; Pg 12 ©Norbert Schuller Baupi @ Wiki; Pg 13 ©hudiemm; Pg 14 ©ELyrae; ©Chuck Wagner; Pg 17 ©Brian Gratwicke; Pg 19, 20 & 22 ©Jean and Fred; Pg 23 ©Sari ONeal; Pg 24 ©davemhuntphotography; Pg 26 ©Judy Gallagher; Pg 28 ©ePhotocorp; Pg 30 ©Cornel Constantin; ©Ingo Rechenberg @ wiki

Edited by: Kim Thompson
Cover and interior design by: Kathy Walsh

Library of Congress PCN Data

Spiders Are Acrobats! And Other Strange Facts / Gary Sprott
(That's Wild!)
ISBN 978-1-73161-727-9 (hardcover)
ISBN 978-1-73161-251-9 (softcover)
ISBN 978-1-73161-739-2 (e-Book)
ISBN 978-1-73161-751-4 (ePub)
Library of Congress Control Number: 2019932373

Rourke Educational Media
Printed in the United States of America,
North Mankato, Minnesota